Contents

Foreword		2
Preface		3

THE FAMILY Past *and* Present

chapter 1	Ideals *and* Realities	4
chapter 2	*To 'Live Together' or to* Marry?	7
chapter 3	Divorce	15
chapter 4	Children *and* Young People	20
chapter 5	Other Pressures	34
chapter 6	Crisis *and* Commitment	38

WORKING NOW *for the* Future

chapter 7	Public Policy	42
chapter 8	*The* Bible—Basis *for* a Christian Response	46
chapter 9	Christian Responses *to the* Crisis	53
Appendix		69

Credits

Design concept by Mark Blackadder

Photographs courtesy of:

Hugh Brown
Donald Clements
Philip Malloch
Ann Nelson

Typeset in Palatino and Helvetica.

Printed and **bound** in Scotland by
H K Clarkson & Sons Ltd, Young Street,
West Calder, West Lothian.

Published on behalf of:
The BOARD of SOCIAL RESPONSIBILITY
of The CHURCH of SCOTLAND
by SAINT ANDREW PRESS
121 George Street, Edinburgh EH2 4YN

Copyright © The BOARD of SOCIAL
RESPONSIBILITY
of The CHURCH of SCOTLAND 1992

British Library in Cataloguing Data
A catalogue record for this book is
available from the British Library.
ISBN 0861531574

All rights reserved. No part of this publication may be reproduced or transmitted in any form or by any means, electronic or mechanical, including photocopy, recording, or information storage and retrieval system, without permission in writing from the publisher. This book is sold, subject to the condition that it shall not, by way of trade or otherwise, be lent, re-sold, hired out or otherwise circulated without the publisher's prior consent.

Foreword

In 1990, the Board of Social Responsibility re-activated its Study Group on Family Matters, asking it to provide a means of consultation with the Panel on Doctrine's working party on the doctrine of marriage, and *to commend and support the Christian ideal of the family, while taking a compassionate and realistic approach to those in different circumstances.*

The Study Group completed its work in December 1991. On 19th May 1992, the General Assembly of the Church of Scotland received the Board's report on family matters, and unanimously agreed, on the motion of the Vice-Convener of the Panel *'to commend it to the whole church for study and action.'*

We are now delighted to pick up the endorsement of our work by the General Assembly and its Panel on Doctrine, and present the report for general use. It is our earnest prayer that this work will be of real help to all in the Church, and to the many others who share our concerns, although not necessarily our faith.

Rev. Andrew T MacLean
Convener of the Board of Social Responsibility
July 1992

Preface

Welcome to this report. It falls into two parts: where is the family, and where would we like it to be in the future?

The first chapter includes a short, up to date statement of the Christian ideal of marriage and the family. Then we look at three patterns which differ from the ideal: living together without marriage, divorce, and single parenthood. We ask: do such arrangements improve on marriage? What are the effects on children? What are the pressures on teenagers today?

In the second part we propose positive action, not only by employers and those who make public policy, but by ourselves within the church. Christians find God's guidance in the Bible: what does it actually say? How can individuals, families, ministers and the local and national church make a difference?

I would like to thank all the members of the Study Group for their friendship and hard work over the last two years. We set out 'to commend and support the Christian ideal of the family, while taking a compassionate and realistic approach to those in different circumstances'.

If our report helps someone to cope with the pain of family breakdown, or better still to prevent it; if it makes someone more sensitive to the hurts which others feel, or better still moves them to offer practical help; if it encourages someone to offer committed love, or better still makes them aware of God, the source of love, we in the Study Group will feel our work was well worth while.

Rev. Philip R M Malloch
Convener of the Study Group on Family Matters
July 1992

THE FAMILY
PAST and PRESENT

1 IDEALS and REALITIES

The Pace of Change

Each of us has a different understanding of what 'family' means. The last 30 years have seen rapid changes in the structure of family life in Britain. More of the population live alone. Since 1961, the number of single person households has jumped from one eighth of the total to one quarter. Many of these are elderly. Couples with dependent children have formed less than one third of households for over a decade and the proportion continues to fall.

The number of families affected by divorce has risen dramatically. In the early 1950s, 35 couples a week were divorced in Scotland. Now the figure is 236.

The number of infants born to unmarried parents has soared —more than 17,800 in Scotland in 1990, representing 27% of the total number of births, up from 8% in the early 1970s. Many children now live in lone parent households. ('Lone' is the generic term which includes 'single', i.e. never married, 'separated', i.e. still married, 'divorced' and 'widowed.') One in five households in Britain is headed by a lone parent, the proportion having more than trebled since 1961.

Other factors have altered too. More couples 'live together' without being married. More women are involved in economic activity outside the home. Job mobility continues, leaving many families distanced from close relatives.

This is where we are. Should the Church simply accept the changes and go with the tide? The Board of Social Responsibility thinks not. There is great cause for concern.

> 'In the early 1950s, 35 couples a week were divorced in Scotland. Now the figure is 236.

> 'The number of infants born to unmarried parents has soared—more than 17,800 in Scotland in 1990, representing 27% of the total number of births, up from 8% in the early 1970s.'

Needs and the Family

Every person has various needs—physical, emotional, psychological and spiritual. The family lies at the heart of meeting, or failing to meet, those needs. Our relationships have a profound influence in the development of personality. It is through our relationships that our individual identities develop. In particular, the relationships which a person has during childhood are crucial to how he or she will mature as an adult.

Therefore it is important that a child grows up experiencing 'reliable love' (Whitfield). A child needs not only to be fed and clothed but also to be nurtured and accepted, to be given love with commitment. Those needs do not stop at childhood; they continue through adolescence and into adulthood. Unless a child is on the receiving end of such committed love during childhood, then he or she will have difficulty in accepting, giving and sustaining such love in adulthood.

Christians claim that there is a new depth to their sense of identity through a relationship with Jesus Christ, the Lord. When someone comes to faith in Christ, the relationship with Him becomes central. But such a person will still have to come to terms with, and cope with, the legacy of earlier relationships.

So what happens within the family of a child is important, not only for that child at the time, but also for the succeeding generations, as he or she reaches adulthood and in turn becomes a parent.

'growing up'?

'It is important that a child grows up experiencing "reliable love".' (Whitfield)

Sensitive Concern

The Board believes that the changes in family structures in Scotland have serious implications for the nurture of children, and therefore serious implications for the future of our society.

None of us is perfect, none of us has had a perfect upbringing, none of us has perfect family relationships. This makes it difficult to tackle issues relating to the family. They are sensitive issues. They touch people in their very hearts. It is hard to say 'that is not good' or 'that should not be', when in so doing someone may be touched on the raw, and pained. But the sensitivity of the issues should not make us shirk from them. It is vital that they are addressed both within the Church and in society at large.

' … none of us has perfect family relationships.'

Ideals

Marriage in the Western world remains popular, with over 90% of men and women choosing to marry. The UK has the joint highest marriage rate in the European Community. Most people in Scotland marry. Marriage reached a peak of popularity in the early 1970s when 70% of Scottish women were married. Now 55% are, with over 34,600 new marriages being formed in Scotland in 1990.

New marriages start with hopes and dreams of love, happiness and life-long security. Western society today has extremely high expectations of marriage. The best features of traditional Judaeo–Christian marriage—life-long intention, faithfulness, and the eventual prospect of children—are not forgotten. In addition couples expect sexual happiness, mutual emotional satisfaction and the opportunity for personal growth. Since expectations are higher, disappointment is all the greater if the ideal is not realised. The Board offers **a contemporary statement of the Christian ideal of marriage and family**:

'New marriages start with hopes and dreams of love, happiness and life-long security.'

- One man and one woman freely give themselves to each other in the life-long commitment of marriage, making promises before God and other people. They express their love for each other in action, caring for one another and helping each other to continue to mature.
- In this context of trusting security, they engage in sexual

relations, knowing that any child who may be conceived will be welcome within the family.
* As a couple, each parent provides for their children, physically, emotionally, mentally and spiritually. They aim to help each child to grow in all these areas, so each dependant can reach full maturity, taking his or her place as a dependable adult in society, caring for the next and the previous generations.

The problem with such an ideal is not in the stating of it, but in the living of it. Our world is not ideal, and we are not ideal people.

2 To 'LIVE TOGETHER' or to MARRY?

The Social Scene

The 1991 census statistics are awaited with interest, but even on estimated figures there has been a great rise in the popularity of living together, especially among younger people. In the UK in 1989, 6% of all people aged 16–59 were cohabiting, with peak figures of 15% for men aged 25–29 and 15% for women aged 20–24. Comparative figures with 1979 are available only for women aged 18–49. In that age group, 8% of single women were cohabiting in 1979 compared with 20% in 1988. For all women in the age group the increase was from 3% to 8%.

Public attitudes have changed. Living together has become socially acceptable. Not only so, there is considerable pressure to do likewise, particularly among young people.

The Church has had little impact in stemming this tide. Nor is it immune to its influence. Many young people inside and outside the Church ask, 'Well, what's wrong with it anyway?'

Some Christians accept the trend as inevitable and seem to concede that there may be nothing wrong with living together. Others hanker after some lost ideal but feel powerless to influence

'Living together has become socially acceptable.'

any positive return to it. There is also a problem for parents who risk alienating their offspring if they seek to 'take a stand' and pronounce their non-approval of a live-in relationship.

Living together isn't new

For centuries the Church, and later the State, has had to face the fact that some people do not follow the recognised rules for 'regular marriage.' Indeed, in Scotland, two types of 'irregular marriage' were legal until 1940 (and a third still is: marriage by cohabitation with habit and repute). In one type of irregular marriage, the couple themselves simply declared that they took each other as husband and wife; there was no need for the presence of a cleric or witnesses. In the other, the marriage was constituted by a promise to marry at a future date followed by sexual intercourse on the faith of that promise.

In some of today's cohabitations, it may be that the couple have made a commitment similar to that envisaged in these irregular marriages, even although it is not technically called 'marriage.' (The historical base is quite different in England.)

Rejecting Marriage ...

... as outmoded

Some people may think that marriage fails to give any meaningful status or rights. They may consider that it would place unwelcome restraints on them.

In fact, the law relating to married couples has changed greatly in the last few decades, particularly in the mid 1980s. A married couple are now equal partners in the eyes of the law. Gone are the days when a husband had the right to dictate where the family home should be, was responsible for his wife's tax affairs, was exempt from a charge of rape. A woman now has the same obligation to support her husband financially as he has always had to support her. There is a legal presumption that any

'A married couple are now equal partners in the eyes of the law.'

household goods obtained during a marriage belong equally to the husband and wife. After a divorce, the emphasis now is on encouraging 'a clean break' financially, re-allocating family assets, with continuing maintenance payments only for children.

These legal changes have been made to reflect changing attitudes, especially towards women. Do some couples choose not to marry, not because marriage *is* outmoded, but because they have an outmoded *view* of the legal consequences?

What of the legal consequences of choosing to 'live together' rather than to marry? A cohabitee has limited rights in the eyes of the law. Neither has any rights to the other's property on death, unless they have made wills. There are no special legal rules to help sort out their affairs on a split up. If they have children, the father has no parental rights unless he applies to the courts. The last thing that many couples contemplating cohabitation may wish to consider are the legal implications. But these may prove to be important to them.

Historically, the rules for 'regular marriage' were made by the Church as it controlled marriage. More recently Parliament has set the rules. The aim is to ensure that an individual's status is certain. Then, his or her rights and responsibilities are clear.

That question remains pertinent today. What rights and responsibilities ought to flow from an arrangement which is not regular marriage? The issue is currently being addressed by the Scottish Law Commission and the Child Care Law Review. If the Church wishes to have a voice then it must arrange to do so. Detailed consideration of these rights and responsibilities is beyond the scope of this Report.

... as too costly

Some couples may reject marriage because of the financial costs and procedures involved in 'getting married.' The present rules date from 1977. Two types of regular marriage are possible, both preceded by civil preliminaries involving the local registrar. The

'The last thing many couples contemplating cohabitation consider are the legal implications.'

ceremony may be conducted either by an authorised religious celebrant or by the registrar. The former may be held anywhere but the latter must be in the registrar's office (unless one of the couple is seriously ill).

Fifty-nine per cent of marriages in Scotland in 1990 were 'religious' and 41% civil. The percentage of civil marriages (introduced in 1940) has risen from only 18% in 1961. Church of Scotland marriages accounted for 56% of the total in 1961 and for 41% in 1990, but that figure has remained comparatively steady since 1978.

Is it possible that there is insufficient flexibility in these arrangements? Some may find the one too expensive and the other too abrupt. Or some may want the ceremonial of the church service but not the religious element. Perhaps the time is right to consider an alternative type of civil ceremony, possibly using a different type of official, which could be conducted in surroundings offering more sense of ceremonial than a registry office.

... as a bad risk

Some people reject marriage because they have direct experience of a 'failed' marriage, their own or their parents. They believe that in some way the lesser commitment of cohabitation will protect them from pain. Living together is seen as giving the freedom to separate, 'with no strings attached.'

However, the indications are that the psychological effects of splitting up after 'living together' are not significantly different from those on separation after marriage for the same period. Obviously, there is no formal legal procedure, but there may still be financial and property implications. There may have been children of the union. The couple must face the likelihood that a split up will involve intense pain and feelings of separation and abandonment, whatever their initial hopes that it might be pain free.

Couples who live together should not be under an illusion that doing so will free them of problems should they decide to separate.

'Living together is seen as giving the freedom to separate, "with no strings attached."'

'Cohabiting appears to some to be a shortcut to happiness, to offer the freedom of a single life and the pleasures of marriage without the risks and complexities of legal commitment. But, in practice, it opens up a whole new set of problems.'

(Church of Scotland *Family Matters Report* 1981)

Living together ...

... as a 'trial'

Some couples choose to live together as a preliminary to possible marriage. This was the course chosen by an estimated 50% of couples who married in Britain in 1989, compared to 37% in the early 1980s and only 4% in the late 1960s.

Some may regard their living together as a trial marriage. The argument often is that this is to check out their compatibility for 'the real thing.' For others, it is almost as if a period of living together has become a stage in the courtship period. A couple 'go out together', possibly 'sleep together' and then decide to 'live together.' They may or may not 'get engaged.' Then ultimately, they 'marry.' They have already made their commitment to one another and are married in all but name, but postpone the public ritual and celebration.

Is there any evidence that marriages following a period of cohabitation have a better chance of enduring? On the contrary, striking new evidence is emerging from the *General Household Survey*:

'From the limited data available, there are signs that for men first married under the age of 30, unions which began with cohabitation and proceeded to first marriage were *more* likely to end within 10 years than first marriages without a period of premarital cohabitation. The contrast for women was weaker.'

(1989 Survey, published 1991)

Others who have 'a trial' before marriage are those who have been married before. Take all marriages begun between 1980 and 1984: if this was the first marriage for both partners, 26% had lived together first; if at least one of the partners had been married before, 70% had lived together first.

For them there may be the very real feeling of 'once bitten, twice shy.' Many people are reluctant to enter a new relationship, having gone through the trauma of marital breakdown. They want to test out the partnership first before committing themselves. The difficulty here is the very question of commitment. How genuine can 'the trial' be, if a mutual commitment is not made? Can the arrangement allow for the giving and receiving of unconditional, reliable love? The very uncertainty can contribute to the misunderstandings which in turn lead to the break-up.

... as a stop-gap

Some couples live together because they want to delay settling down or because they think 'it makes sense' to share resources. There is certainly a trend for later marriage. In Scotland, the average age at which people married reached a low in the 1970s of 22.5 years for women and 24.3 years for men. In 1990, the average age of a first marriage was 26.8 years for men and 25.1 years for women (similar to the average ages recorded in the late nineteenth and early twentieth centuries). In the 20–24 age group 57.1% had married status in 1971, but only 26.4% in 1990.

It may well be wise to counsel young people to delay marriage. The correlation between teenage marriage and resulting divorce is well documented. It is appropriate to delay making the commitment of marriage until one is more fully mature.

However, in today's society, the consequence of that delay is that more people have premarital relationships. Knowing that our personalities and identities are greatly influenced by our previous relationships, these must have an implication for the eventual marriage partnership. These previous relationships, short or long, will have an effect on the marriage relationship which the couple will have to face and live with.

In addition, there are a whole range of health factors which are heightened by the number of sexual partners, and the age at which sexual experience begins. If a person wants to avoid sexually transmitted diseases, the safest route is to have only one partner for life—which is what traditional marriage offers. Any other route makes possible the sharing of infection, not just resources.

... since 'it won't affect the children'

Some couples feel no need to marry since children born 'out of wedlock' are no longer stigmatised. It is right that a child should not be penalised in the eyes of the law or by society because his parents are not married. Again there has been a major shift in public attitudes; and the stigma, and indeed the term 'illegitimate', have all but gone. For centuries, a child's rights in Scots law depended on whether or not he was legitimate, but since 1986 children have had equality in the eyes of the law whether legitimate or not.

That being so, are there other implications for a child if his parents are living together unmarried? What of the 'security' aspect? Is that child assured of a stable family unit? Undoubtedly, some couples do create enduring, stable, loving relationships without ever formalising the bond in marriage. They need to be commended and supported. However, others do not. (Sadly, given current divorce rates, a child in a marriage setting cannot be assured of a stable family unit either.)

... since we *can't* marry

Some couples live together because they are not free to marry. This is increasingly common, as more and more marriages break down. 'Living together' is most prevalent among couples where one or both has been married before. In 1989, 43% of divorced men were estimated to be cohabiting and 28% of separated men. The figures for women were 26% of divorcees and 15% of separated.

> 'If a person wants to avoid sexually transmitted diseases, the safest route is to have only one partner for life ...'

Caution is called for. It may be unwise to get involved in a new relationship with unresolved hurts and issues from a previous marriage when the divorce process and the individual healing process are still incomplete.

From a Christian point of view there is also the whole issue of living with someone who is already married. The word 'adultery' has almost disappeared from contemporary vocabulary (except as evidence for establishing breakdown of marriage). Has society truly moved to a point of acceptance of living with someone else's partner? We think not. A MORI poll conducted in 1989 found that 70% of those interviewed put faithfulness top of the list for what is important in a marriage.

Christians should be clear. **Adultery is wrong**. It is deeply hurtful and destructive (see chapter 8).

Marriage is best

In considering the various forms of 'living together' and marriage, the Board affirms that marriage is best. In chapter 8 we shall show how the Bible declares the worth of a life-long marriage relationship. From the fields of history, sociology and psychology, some would say that the most likely setting for personal fulfilment is consistent with the marriage ideal.

If a man and woman believe themselves to have mutual, committed, unconditional love and support, they may see no reason for a marriage ceremony. Publicly affirmed promises are however important. It is in the nature of love to want to bind itself, to make a pledge. The promises made at a wedding are an expression of a solemn pledge, to love and to cherish, for better for worse, for richer for poorer, in sickness and in health. They express commitment.

'But the vow or bond has a secondary function .... The pledge acts as a restraint upon our weakness. It gives us power when we are at our weakest. This is what G K Chesterton calls "the law of the second wind." In every human endeavour of any value and significance there comes a moment when we are tempted to desert because the first, fine, careless rapture has passed. It is here that faithfulness to the pledge carries us, till we get our second wind and go on again with restored enthusiasm.' (Holloway)

'the start of a shared journey'

The ceremony of marriage marks the start of a shared journey. Ideally, husband and wife will sustain each other in their day to day living, will help heal one another's past and present wounds, will respond to the growth and change in one another. People respond positively to a love that can be trusted, that is committed, that is reliable. **'Reliable love is one hundred times stronger than conditional affection'** (Whitfield).

3 DIVORCE

Marriage is no longer life-long for a significant proportion of the population. In 1988, one in five of British men in their 40s had been through a divorce, and of women in their 30s and 40s one fifth had also been divorced.

Divorce rates rose dramatically between the mid 1960s and the early 1980s, although they have levelled out in recent years. The UK has the second highest divorce rate in the European Community after Denmark. There were 12,272 divorces in Scotland in 1990—over 111,000 in the last decade. In England and Wales around 151,000 couples are divorced every year.

'There were 12,272 divorces in Scotland in 1990 ...'

There is a trend towards higher percentages of first marriages dissolving within ten years. For example, 9% of men who were married for the first time in 1960–64 had separated within ten years, but 20% of those who were married for the first time in 1975–79.

Being divorced does not necessarily lead to a rejection of married life. Most divorcees remarry. Of those first divorced in the mid 1970s, an estimated 60% of women and 77% of men had remarried within 10 years. Those most likely to be in their second or subsequent marriage are men in their 40s and 50s and women in their late 30s or 40s. Of those getting married in Scotland in 1990, about 20% of both men and women had been married before. Unfortunately, experience of an earlier marriage does not guarantee that second marriages will succeed. Divorces of persons previously divorced accounted for 12% of all divorces in 1990 compared with 7% in 1980.

Divorce Law Reform in Scotland

Changes in the law have made it less complicated to get a divorce. In Scotland, all divorces used to be heard in the Court of Session in Edinburgh. Now, they can be processed locally in the sheriff court, often without a hearing, simply on the basis of prepared statements.

Before 1976, divorce was firmly linked to the concept of 'fault': adultery, desertion, cruelty. Now the emphasis is on 'irretrievable breakdown', although adultery, desertion and 'cruelty' (re-defined as 'unreasonable behaviour') remain as indicators to show that a marriage has indeed broken down irretrievably. There is no minimum period which must elapse before such an action of divorce can be brought.

Irretrievable breakdown can also be shown if the couple live apart for a period—two years if both agree to a divorce, 5 years if one does not. Two years separation with consent is currently the basis for over two-fifths of Scottish divorces (44% in 1990—up from 24% in 1980).

'Most divorcees remarry.'

'In divorce, the emphasis is on "irretrievable breakdown" ...'

The Board has not had the opportunity to consider in detail the effects of divorce law reform on divorce statistics, nor the current proposals for further changes in divorce law. The English Law Commission suggests radical reform—divorce after a period of notice, with no grounds or period of separation required. The Scottish Law Commission has rather recommended a reduction of the separation periods to one year and two years, considering that the present law encourages people to 'create' a fault ground in order to get a divorce sooner than the two year separation basis allows. The Scottish Law Commission's proposal was resisted by the Church of Scotland. [It was dropped from the Law Reform (Miscellaneous Provisions) (Scotland) Bill 1990 for political reasons.]

The Church was closely involved in the debate at the time of the major divorce law reform of the 1970s. As the recommendations recently produced for England may influence the course of reform in Scotland, the Board intends to study the issues and report.

Living through Divorce

Divorce is not simply the severing of the legal tie of marriage. It is part of a process, beginning before a couple separate and going on beyond the date of the divorce decree. However 'amicable' the divorce proceedings may be, 'breaking up is hard to do.' The implications of the split-up can be painful and difficult, emotionally, financially, practically and spiritually. In bringing 'a Christian perspective' to this subject of divorce, the Board not only comments on the theological and social considerations, but also remembers our calling to reach out in love.

Many readers will know the depths of experience of living through separation and divorce. For some, it may be a 'faith provoking' or a 'growing' experience but few would dispute the soul-searching, pain and loneliness first involved. The sense of

'However "amicable" the divorce proceedings may be, "breaking up is hard to do".'

betrayal, fear, and loss experienced at the ending of a relationship should not be underestimated.

Modern divorce law may well have helped reduce in part the stresses associated with marital breakup. For some, domestic violence or the threat of it makes separation inevitable and essential. Law reforms, especially the provision of exclusion orders, have been helpful in offering women some protection in such situations.

> '... the very intimacy of the marriage relationship may raise unresolved conflicts or insecurities from childhood.'

There is a concern, however, that the ease with which a divorce can be obtained means that for some people, divorce is taken as the way out, when there may be a need to address some deep-seated personal question. It can be that the very intimacy of the marriage relationship raises unresolved conflicts or insecurities from childhood. For that person, unless the fundamental problems are sorted out, the prospect is that he or she will enter another relationship which may prove no more satisfactory.

Counselling

Therefore, it may be that for some couples an early counselling opportunity would help them to take another look at their relationship and to try to deal with the problems, individually and as a couple. Any future legislation ought to allow time for counselling prior to a final decision. The Board's counselling services at Simpson House, Edinburgh and the Tom Allan Centre in Glasgow offer direct counselling provision and also courses to train counsellors. Marriage Guidance and others also offer counselling services.

> 'It is important not to underestimate the stresses other factors have on marriage.'

In mentioning the personal relationship aspect of marriage break-up, it is important not to underestimate the stresses that other factors have on marriages. In two polls in 1989 (Gallup and MORI), three quarters of those interviewed considered that financial problems were the main contributory factor to marriage breakdown. Much more could be alluded to: the problems arising out of work or domestic pressures, absence of support from extended family, unemployment and redundancy, credit and debt, house repossession and homelessness; and the media portrayal of a society in which happiness is linked to material prosperity.

The stress of marital breakdown is not confined to the couple. For effects on children, see chapter 4. There are implications for the extended family too, particularly often for grandparents. Individual families may not look beyond themselves but, as citizens, we have a responsibility to consider the wider effects of divorce on society at large.

The 'Costs' of Divorce

Marital breakdown and lone-parenting are costly to society in terms of ill-health, absenteeism and homelessness, as well as in the legal costs, social security benefits, and health and social service demands.

> 'The general health of those who are married is better than that of their single, widowed, divorced or separated counterparts; and these differences are greater for men than for women. In the stress league, marital breakdown is ranked second only to the death of a much-loved spouse. It ranks far above unemployment or imprisonment, and it hits men harder. Separation or divorce increases the likelihood of a person becoming a psychiatric in-patient by a factor of seven for women and fourteen for men. Their chances of going to prison, committing suicide, or dying—from heart or other disease or road accidents—are all greatly increased.'   (Argyle)

More working days are lost by separated or divorced people than by staff who are married or single. Time is lost, not just through ill-health, but by employees having to take days off to see solicitors, counsellors etc. A recent estimate put the loss caused by absenteeism and impaired efficiency resulting from marriage breakdown at £200 million a year.

Marital breakdown is a factor in homelessness. Many young

people do not have a 'home' to which to return. They come from split families where both parents may have new partners with young children, constituting a new family unit.

More men than women re-marry. Growing numbers of ex-wives risk financial disadvantage in old age unless they re-marry or have accumulated sufficient pension entitlement on their own. 'By the year 2025 it is estimated that 1 in 8 women and 1 in 11 men will have broken up with their spouse without marrying again. The number of elderly divorcees will rise four-fold if present divorce rates continue.' Clearly this has implications for the future care of old people (Family Policy Study Centre Report 1991).

Divorce is estimated to cost the UK £1,300 million a year in legal costs, social security and health service bills, welfare and child-care payments. The direct annual economic cost to tax-payers of special provisions for lone parenthood is estimated at around £4,000 million a year. Dr Jack Dominian, Director of One Plus One, calls marriage breakdown 'a private agony and a public cost.'

Even before taking into account the effects on children, society must face up to the costs of divorce.

4 CHILDREN *and* YOUNG PEOPLE

Children's welfare is high up the priority scale in our legal system. This is right in view of the vulnerability of children, and since they are the future of the nation.

As already stated, so much of our experience as adults is rooted in our childhood experiences that it is vital that we look at the implications for children of the changing shape of family structures today.

Some children are born knowing no father. Others begin life with two parents but end up with only one through death, separation or divorce. Then, if a parent marries or remarries, a child has a step parent and perhaps step brothers and sisters. These new parental relationships may be formalised in marriage, or long term live-in arrangements, or transitory.

Almost one-fifth of families with children in Britain are headed by a lone parent—a three-fold increase in 30 years (19% in 1990 compared with 6% in 1961). This is one of the highest percentages in Europe, though less than the USA (25%). The vast majority of these lone parents are women. Only 2% of all families with dependent children are headed by a lone father.

'safe in the arms of love'

Of course, it has always been possible that families lose one or both parents through death. One hundred years ago with higher rates of parental death, there were as many lone parents in relation to the population as there are now. There were even more in wartime. Today, however, 60% of lone parents are divorced and nearly 30% have never married.

Children born outside Marriage

The trend

The proportion of births which occurred outside marriage rose significantly over the 20 year period from 1968, particularly between 1985 and 1987. Seven per cent of all UK births were outside marriage in 1968, 15% in 1985 and 23% in 1987.

In Scotland the graph is also climbing steeply. Eight per cent of births were to unmarried parents in the period 1970–74, 10% in 1975–1980, 14% in 1980–84, 22% in 1985–89. In 1990, over one-quarter of live births in Scotland were to unmarried mothers: 17,873 babies out of a total of 65,973. Apart from a short period in the late 1970s, in terms of numbers, most births outside marriage since 1946 have been to women in their early 20s.

These are births to 'unmarried parents.' This does not neces-

'In 1990, over one-quarter of live births in Scotland were to unmarried mothers.'

sarily mean 'lone' parent as some parents may be living together. There is an increasing trend for couples to register a birth jointly and a growing percentage of those couples register the same address.

The upward trend is across all age bands. But the younger the mother, the more likely she is to be unmarried. In the age band 25–29, 17% of births are to unmarried mothers. In the age band 20–24, 40% are to unmarried mothers. Among the under 20s, 80% of births are to unmarried mothers. In terms of actual numbers, fewer teenagers now have babies. In 1990 the number of births to teenage mothers in Scotland was 5,600 compared to an average of 9,000 each year in the late 1960s and early 1970s. But, the proportion where the parents are unmarried has increased hugely: 80% in 1990 compares with 24% in the period 1970–74, 45% in 1980–84.

This reflects the downward trend in the number of teenage marriages which in turn is part of the trend towards later marriage. In 1973 the percentage of men marrying in Scotland before they were 20 reached a peak of over 12%. Since then the rate has dropped annually, to 2% in 1990. For women, over 30% of those who married in 1966 were under 20 (the peak year). By 1990 just under 7% married as teenagers.

Single mothers

Contraception is readily available. Evidently, some single women consciously *choose* to have a baby. For them the baby is planned or at least desired and welcome. For other single mothers, pregnancy is entirely unplanned and the resulting responsibilities are totally unsought. Despite years of education in schools about sex, pregnancy and contraception, the evidence suggests that many young people simply do not link them together. 'Lots of other girls get pregnant but it won't happen to me.'

Teenage mothers, as mentioned above, are now much less likely to marry the father of their child. There may still be a stigma attached to being an unmarried mother, but society has become less disapproving. Also, it is no longer thought necessary to marry 'for the sake of the child.' Illegitimacy has few legal consequences.

Not marrying the father has its advantages, given the relative instability of youthful marriages. In 50% of Scottish divorces in 1990 one or both of the parties was under 21 at the time of the marriage.

However, that then means—on the bare statistics—that the mother is alone and that the child knows no father. Of course, in some cases, the father may have contact with the child—may indeed be living with the child's mother. In other cases, there may be a good network of family support for mother and child. Many mothers are able to obtain houses of their own because they have a child; but that increases the risk of a new problem—isolation.

There are other implications, particularly for the teenage mother —the loss of her 'freedom' as a young person to continue her education, or pursue a career, or go out with her friends; the loss of the final years of her own childhood, the responsibility thrust upon her of bringing up a child when she has barely reached maturity herself.

On the wider perspective, social deprivation must be recognised as a significant factor in the cycle of teenage births. For example, a report produced for Lothian Region based on birth data from 1980–89 reveals that half the mothers in Craigmillar and Pilton (areas of social deprivation in Edinburgh) were unmarried and one in every four mothers was under 20. In Braids/Fairmilehead (a more affluent area) only one in every 34 mothers was single and only one in every 213 births was to a teenager (*Social Indicator Analysis for Lothian*: Birth Data 1980–89). People who live and work in such areas are recognising the new scale of teenage pregnancy as a real problem. Part of the difficulty may be boredom, especially just after leaving school. The desire for a bit of excitement can lead to sex and unexpected pregnancy. Behind that, those working in such areas suggest that lack of self confidence and lack of self-esteem are contributory factors. Some of these young women feel that there is a positive status to be gained from becoming a mother; others feel that there is more stigma to having an abortion than to being an unmarried mother.

Do children need fathers?

In law, a child is entitled to financial support from both his parents whether they are married or not. However, a father does not have automatic parental rights if he is not married to his child's mother. He is not entitled to share in his child's parenting, although he is obliged (in theory at least) to contribute to his or her financial support. The Scottish Law Commission may recommend a change in the law to give such fathers automatic parental rights, or alternatively to allow a couple to agree that he will have such rights.

'a stabilising influence'?

' ... a father does not have automatic parental rights if he is not married to his child's mother.'

Attitudes have been influenced by various factors including women's rights, changing male/female relationships, an economic shift from men to women and advances in reproductive technologies.

Some say that one committed parent is all a child needs. Certainly, a great many adults, some quite young, are bringing up children single-handedly in a highly committed way, juggling work and home, managing the finances, providing for emotional needs and so on. None of this Report is in any sense meant to discourage existing single parents, often making commendable efforts to do their best for their child(ren).

However, there are findings that children of single-parent families tended to have more illness, to die earlier, to do less well at school, to suffer more unemployment, to be more prone to deviance and crime, and to repeat the cycle of unstable parenting from which they themselves had been formed (Professor Halsey, Emeritus Professor of Social Administration, Oxford 1991).

It is widely held by educationalists and others working for the welfare of children that the family comprising a man and woman and their children works best for children. Boys and girls need both men and women to rear them, for role-modelling, wider stimulation and the opportunity to perceive facets of gender difference.

It is striking that in areas where many children are in families 'without fathers', a role played by good neighbours and the wider family is that of a 'father figure' to the children.

Some children even in 'intact' families do not have close contact with their fathers, whether through work pressures, disinterest or other causes. This too can have a detrimental effect on the children. The shadow of child abuse also affects many children, with and 'without' fathers.

Children whose Parents Divorce

Over 9,500 children in Scotland saw their parents divorce in 1990.

It is estimated that 1 in 5 children in the United Kingdom will experience a parental divorce by the age of 16. If current trends continue towards the end of the century, only 1 in 2 children will experience 'traditional' family life with two natural parents throughout their childhood.

Forty-seven per cent of Scottish divorces in 1990 were of couples with children under 16. The number of children whose parents divorce is falling (down 13% since 1980) but a rising percentage of divorces involve children under five years old, up from 18% in 1980 to 24% in 1990.

What happens to the children ... ?

Another sensitive question: many readers will have experienced divorce. Many adults and children may have come through the experience 'and out the other side', having done the best in the circumstances with no apparent adverse long-term effects on anyone.

It is important, however, to consider the evidence that is available. There are significant indicators of a tendency to disturbance in young children following their parents' separation.

... in the short term ?

Speaking of the short term effects of marital break-up, Gerald Caplan, Emeritus Professor of psychiatry, Harvard University, reported in the British Medical Journal in 1986:

> 'There is compelling evidence that divorce exerts a harmful effect on children, over and above the psychological damage that may have been caused by the discord between the parents that led to the separation .... Almost all children are greatly upset by the break-up of their home. For many months they react with sadness, depression, anger, regression, feelings of deprivation and insecurity, and emotional conflicts that often find expression in such bodily symptoms as nocturnal enuresis (bed-wetting), headache or abdominal pain. These psychological reactions induced by stress often last for a year or more before the children adjust to the major changes in their home life.'

Some people assume that children get over this with few long term effects. Until the mid 1980s, research concentrated on the damaging effects on the children in poor marriages.

... in the long term?

However, evidence is accumulating of more difficulties in the long term. The research includes a follow-up study of children born in 1946, involving regular contact with them through their adult lives.

> 'Delinquency by the age of 21 was significantly higher among young people of both sexes whose parents had split up, particularly if the divorce had occurred while the child was aged

'There is compelling evidence that divorce exerts a harmful effect on children ...'

under five years. The experience of parental separation was also a risk to educational attainment, which carried with it the associated risk to socio-economic achievement in adulthood. This was, however, not so among children who had experienced the death of a parent; in some instances they seemed to do even better than might have been expected. Men who as children experienced separation of their parents were significantly more likely than others to be unemployed, and were also significantly more likely to be single or divorced.'

(Michael Wadsworth and colleagues, *Family Practice*, 1990)

The report did not have data about the quality of parental relationships in the families where the parents stayed married. This might have revealed a similar level of emotional problems, and subsequent risk, among children whose parents had a consistently bad relationship. However, such children would not have had to cope with the stress associated with moving house and/or schools following marriage break-up. Neither would they have had to cope with the risk of reduction in income associated with the divorce.

Wadsworth concluded that although the evidence did not show a simple causal link between separation of parents and later life problems for their children, it did reveal a sufficient level of increased risk to merit concern in individual care and in the design of policy.

Professor Caplan has also reported the effects of divorce on children at a later stage, including increased rates of births outside marriage, divorce, depression, emotional problems, gastric ulcer, colitis and hypertension.

Some studies suggest that the effects of a divorce are particularly long-lasting if a child is aged under six at the time of the divorce. This is of particular concern in the light of the increasing proportion of young children in Scotland whose parents divorce.

'... the effects of a divorce are particularly long-lasting if a child is aged under six at the time of the divorce.'

An 'invisible' effect of divorce on children is the hidden fear felt by their friends: *'Will my parents be next?'*

It used to be thought that an unhappy marriage was always the worst scenario for children and that it was better for such parents to divorce. The recent evidence indicates the extent to which children suffer during and following divorce. This data must be taken into account by those who are formulating divorce law reform. It may be that there is merit after all in encouraging people to stay together for the sake of the children. At the very least, unhappy couples need to be made aware that a divorce will not *solve* their problems, but merely *exchange* one set of problems for another.

What happens to family income?

One must be careful not to deduce that parental separation in itself is the cause of all the difficulties mentioned. A significant factor with regard to later problems can be lack of family income. Divorce disadvantages children financially.

The principal source of income for many lone families is state support. Less than half of lone mothers received financial support from a former partner. Legal measures are being introduced to try to improve the record of making fathers pay.

Lone mothers are less likely to be employed. This may relate to their family responsibilities and the inadequacy of alternative practical support for the children. Britain has one of the lowest rates of child care provision in Europe. Forty-four per cent of lone mothers are in paid work compared to 62% of married or cohabiting mothers. Although lone mothers are more likely than other mothers to be working full time, the trend is downwards—17% of lone mothers worked full time in 1987–89 compared to 22% in 1977–79. A steady quarter of lone mothers work part time. Far more divorced (58%) and separated (46%) mothers work than single mothers (27%).

The income of lone parents is significantly less than that of other households with children. For example, in 1989, 52% of lone

'Divorce disadvantages children financially.'

parents had total gross income of less than £100 per week. Only 5% of other households with dependent children had as little. At the other end of the scale, only 8% of lone parent households had total gross income above £350 per week compared to 46% of other households with dependent children.

Lone parent families are more likely than other families to rent their homes. In 1987/88, 54% of lone parents rented from a local authority compared to only 18% of other families. Some commentators say: 'In many studies of child development, apparent differences between children of one-parent and two-parent families disappear once allowance is made for social class, poverty, poor housing and environment' (Gingerbread and The National Council for One Parent Families, *Times* 5/8/88). Undoubtedly, 'unemployment and single parenthood bring high risks of poverty' (*Poverty the Facts*, CPAG 1990). Whatever the extent or the source of the hardship, children of lone parents are disadvantaged economically.

How can we help children in a divorce situation?

Ann Mitchell of Edinburgh University found from her research (*Children in the Middle*, 1985) that children were more distressed by their parents' separation than the parents realised. Her book underlined the vital need for parents to let their children know what is happening, and emphasised the important role of grandparents, teachers and other connected adults during the period of the break-up. Anyone who has contact with a family breaking up should be sensitive to the children's needs, giving them the opportunity to talk, to give vent to their upsets, fears, and uncertainties. Parents should be encouraged to keep their children informed about practical points, such as where they'll be living, when they'll see the parent who's moved out, what will happen about school, what they can tell their friends.

'Anyone who has contact with a family breaking up should be sensitive to the children's needs ...'

Where will the children live?

Custody is a crucial issue when a marriage breaks up. In the majority of cases, divorcing parents agree with whom the children will live. Where there is a dispute, the courts tend to preserve the status quo and award custody to the parent who has looked after the child since the separation (provided this is in the best interests of the child). Formal awards of joint custody are unusual in Scotland. Most often, neither party applies for custody. The result is informal joint custody with a lack of clarity over rights and responsibilities. The exact legal implications of an award of custody are currently under consideration by the Scottish Law Commission who recognise that it is important that the parental rights of an absent parent are not removed unnecessarily.

Does keeping in touch matter?

Many couples make arrangements for access, but in practice access may become irregular, particularly if the parents subsequently enter into new family relationships, or even just move house.

A report from the Family Policy Studies Centre has estimated that more than 750,000 children in the UK may have lost contact with their fathers. An estimated one in three children lose contact with the absent parent within two years of a divorce.

There is also evidence to suggest that fathers who were relatively highly involved with and attached to their children during the marriage are more likely to lose contact with their children after divorce, than fathers previously on the periphery of their children's lives. It is suggested that the existing approach to access makes it difficult for such fathers to keep a link which in any way maintains the closeness of their previous bond (*The impact of divorce on Non-custodial fathers*, research by E. Kruck).

Achieving and maintaining links with both parents can be difficult. Yet there is growing evidence that children will cope

'... *more than 750,000 children in the UK may have lost contact with their fathers.*'

better with the trauma of the break-down of their parents' marriage when they can sustain such links.

Conciliation Services have been established throughout Scotland over the last decade with the object of enabling couples to reach amicable agreement on the practical arrangements for their children following separation or divorce. They do not attempt to bring about *reconciliation* between the parents. Conciliators recognise that if parents split up, children do best if they continue to see both parents and the parents communicate well about the children.

A recent report (*Family Conciliation in Scotland*, Scottish Office 1990) indicates that about three quarters of those who used the service found it helpful, both because it helped solve immediate problems, and because it led to an improvement in long term communications between the parents. The report also suggests that conciliation is more likely to be effective where it is attended early, particularly before the couple actually separate.

The work of the Conciliation Service is to be commended. Future research will be required to see whether 'practical parenting plans ' devised in the context of the Service are more likely to be effective in ensuring that contact with an absent parent is maintained.

Serial Families

Over six million adults and children in Britain now live in stepfamilies. 'Serial monogamy' or 'sequential polygamy' are two ways of describing the series of relationships when couples split up and remarry. Increasingly, that is the pattern today.

Children may find themselves in simple or more complex stepfamily situations. The parent with whom they live may make only one new bond, that person becoming the step-parent. Alternatively, there may be a series of live-in relationships with no one final long term choice. Similar patterns may emerge for the absent parent.

The situation may also be confused by the presence within one household of children with the same biological parentage, with one

> '... children will cope better with the trauma of breakdown when they can sustain links with both parents ...'

common biological parent, or with no common biological parent.

A child must adjust to these changing circumstances. Some do so without much apparent difficulty, accepting the newcomer as substitute parent. Others accept the newcomer as their parents' new companion, but not as step-parent: they see their own natural parents as still providing the parenting role (Mitchell).

In many such families there may be warm, loving relationships. However, there are some disturbing indicators of greater risks to children and young people in step-family situations, for example in relation to child abuse, poorer health, poorer school attendance, homelessness, police involvement. Abuse figures need to be treated with caution, as children are more likely to *disclose* abuse by a step-parent than by a natural parent.

It would seem self-evident that children in complicated family arrangements must be subject to greater stress than other children. However, it has proved beyond the scope of this Report to consider the issue of 'serial families' in any depth. Further research on the implications for children will emerge as the pattern of 'serial monogamy' increases.

The Teenage Years

'Some have opportunities unheard of 40 years ago ... others have dificult home situations ... no job ... no prospects of life getting better.'

Many young people have a freedom and independence unknown in previous generations. The influences and pressures on them are varied—e.g. to make some money, to find a job, to choose a career, to experiment sexually. Some have opportunities in education, sport and luxuries unheard of 40 years ago; others have difficult home situations, nowhere to call 'home' at all, no job prospects, no alternatives, no prospects of life getting better. Adolescence is a time of growing sexual awareness. It is also a time of 'kicking the traces' as young people work out their own identities. All sorts of antisocial thoughts and behaviour may be evident as they test the boundaries imposed by adults. Then comes the leaving home experience, a significant one, as a young person wrestles with the conflict of being ready, and yet not ready, to live separately. It is important during those years that a variety of adults are available to the young person, not just their parents, and not just their own peer group. Links between the generations are to be encouraged.

Some adults may think there is already too much teaching about sex and AIDS. Unfortunately, the indications are that education campaigns have failed to change the behaviour of young people. A number of surveys show that many young people have sexual relationships, and that only a minority practise protected sex. In a recent report (Edinburgh University, 13/12/91) researchers found that the interviewees were knowledgeable about the risks posed by AIDS, but did not act on this knowledge. The report concluded that factual information by itself appears insufficient to foster safer sex and warned that unless alternative strategies are adopted the risk of spreading HIV infection remains high. For adolescents entering into sexual relationships, there is not only the risk of AIDS, but also the risk of other sexually transmitted diseases and the heightened risk to sexual health (for example, cervical cancer and pelvic inflammatory disease).

'jumping into the unknown'?

'... many young people have sexual relationships and only a minority practise protected sex.'

Adolescents need to realise that the consequences of their sexual behaviour are not restricted to themselves. There are costs to others and to society. Babies born to teenagers are more likely to be premature and to have a low birthweight. There is a greater risk of death during birth. An unplanned pregnancy interrupts the mother's studies or career prospects. Teenagers, even in work, are likely to be at the lower end of the wage scale. Therefore babies born to teenage mothers will probably be in households with fewer economic assets. There are also issues involving housing and welfare support.

Many unplanned pregnancies are terminated by abortion. In 1989 in Britain there were 181,000 legal abortions, up 30% from 1981. Of these, 4,000 involved girls under 16 and 39,000 involved young women aged 16 to 19.

The most recent Scottish statistics available are for 1988, when the total number of abortions on Scottish residents was 10,854, equivalent to a rate of 9.7 per 1,000 women aged 15–44. The rate has risen from 8.9 per 1,000 in 1985. Of these, 287 were for girls under 16, and another 2,676 for young women aged 16–19. The largest group was those aged 20–24 (3,571). Most of the women were single (66.8%). Cohabiting women were not differentiated.

In communicating with young people, it is important to convey the significance in practical terms of unwanted pregnancies, the risk of disease and so on. However, the Board affirms the importance of right relationships and the special nature of the sexual bond. There are encouraging signs that educators are now suggesting, as the first option for avoiding AIDS, 'not having a sexual relationship.' The Board commends this positive step.

5 OTHER PRESSURES

Changing Work Patterns

The modern two-parent family is increasingly a dual worker family. Fifty-three per cent of married couples with children both work. A growing percentage of married women with dependent children are engaged in economic activity—up from 52% in 1977–79 to 59% in 1987–89.

A significant trend is that each successive group of new mothers returns to the labour market more quickly than the one before. In 1989, 45% of those in work when they became pregnant returned to work within 9 months, compared to 25% ten years before. The proportion returning full-time trebled from 5% to 15% in that period. Thirty per cent of mothers with children under 3 now work, of whom 19% are part-time and 11% full-time.

In Britain a higher proportion of women are active in the labour force than in any other European Community country, except Denmark. It is estimated that women will make up 80% of the total increase in the labour force in the period up to 1995.

These changes are linked to various factors such as increased independence of women, and more women having higher education and then wishing to maintain their career prospects. Sometimes, a married woman may find that few of her contemporaries remain at home; to continue to do so herself would leave her isolated. Many couples, whether or not they have children, find that it is an economic necessity for both partners to earn an income in order to maintain the household.

For some families, however, there is no choice about who will go out to work. Large numbers of people face redundancy or unemployment. In some areas, traditional male employment has been replaced by women starting or continuing work. In other situations, no-one in the family is earning.

Role Changes

There are many pressures for married women with children who return to work. Economic realities may require her to earn to help maintain the household. Yet finding employment which is compatible with home responsibilities can be difficult. As a result, many women take on part-time work. This may be below their capabilities or previous job experience. It may be low paid, with poor working conditions, and part-time workers have few employment rights.

Evidence from the British Social Attitudes Survey suggests that women still perform the majority of domestic chores. The extra demands that this places on women is perhaps still not sufficiently recognised by their men-folk or in society at large.

In areas where women form the majority of the work force, the enforced change in male/female roles is not always easy to accept. Men in particular can find it difficult to adjust to a home-based role with daytime responsibility for the children.

Where both parents are unemployed, the difficulty can be in finding meaningful roles in the home and community, given the restraints of reliance on welfare benefits for income.

On a wider scale, recognition must be given to the adjustments which both men and women must make as changes occur in male and female roles within the workplace and in the home. Couples have to work out for themselves their own understanding of their respective roles, and this takes time.

Time for Families

Whatever the work pattern, it is important that families have appropriate time with one another.

'keeping all the balls in the air'?

In situations of early retirement, redundancy or unemployment, stress can be caused by too much time together. For other families—lone parents, dual workers, busy executives, women who work and maintain the home—sheer lack of time can put pressure on family relationships. Particular difficulties may be faced by couples who work different shifts or where one is employed on a weeks-on/weeks-off pattern like oil-rig workers.

The issue becomes one of priorities. Sometimes, a family has little choice. The demands of a job may mean that work must take precedence over all other responsibilities. Yet, it is vital that family life be given time. If family life is to be maintained, it is important that employers recognise the need to give people the opportunity to make choices about how they will divide family responsibilities and work commitments.

Couples need to make time for one another. Many may have

wider family commitments too, such as caring for elderly or disabled relatives.

They also need time with their children and time together as a family. When working parents have only a short period of contact with their children, they may refer to it as 'quality time' (as distinct from the quantity of time available). However, it is difficult to programme 'quality time', because the quality of the contact depends not on when the parent desires to fit it in, but on when the child needs it and is ready to receive it.

Managing to combine the roles of adequate spouse, responsible parent, supportive relative and committed worker is demanding and requires skilful balancing of roles.

Family Income

Lack of family income can be a major problem for families. It can be the reason why a woman goes into the workplace when the family preference might be for her to be home-based with young children.

It can be one of the reasons why young people end up homeless. Families already under strain face a gap in financial support for their 16 and 17 year olds. For some, this means that these young people are forced out on to the street.

'Families already under strain face a gap in financial support for their 16 to 17 year olds.'

Economic and social deprivation is related to an increased incidence of family problems. For example, greater numbers of child-care referrals and children taken into care involve families dependent on welfare benefits for income. Higher proportions of teenage and extra-marital births are found in areas of social deprivation. Such areas also have a greater incidence of ill-health and higher mortality rates.

Having adequate family income to maintain the household is vital to the well-being of families.

'Having adequate family income is vital.'

6 CRISIS *and* COMMITMENT

Why is Family Life important?

A wide variety of responses might emerge if this question were asked of people in the streets: it's somewhere to come home to—it's somewhere to be close to someone—to share intimacy, husband with wife, parent with child—it's the setting in which to bring up children—it's the essential smaller unit in society.

Studies of human nature suggest that the individual needs love and affirmation. This can be expressed as a cycle of commitment. In a family, if individuals experience reliable love and genuine affirmation of their worth, they are likely to grow in personal confidence with a secure identity. They are more likely then to be able to give mature love and form new bonds. In turn, as they make commitments, reliable promises, they become 'source' people nurturing the growth of others. Commitment involves time and patience.

Love is primarily concerned with an act of will. Our feelings and moods often change. Fulfilling the promises of marriage will call for many conscious decisions to care. To love someone is to commit oneself to sharing life with them. Human relationships are vitally important, even in this consumer-oriented, technological age. Therefore it is essential that society and individuals consider the meaning of 'love', promises, commitment.

The ideal family unit is one in which individuals share and grow, in which they experience safe comings and goings, in which they give and receive unconditional love. From such a family unit come children who become mature adults, able to help create their own loving families. Unconditional love sounds risky. It leaves us open to rejection. But it is also creative, awakening love in return.

It is not always necessary or desirable for the family unit to be self-sufficient. It can be positively valuable for everyone concerned to have links with members of the wider family and community.

> 'In a family, if individuals experience reliable love and genuine affirmation of their worth, they are likely to grow in personal confidence with a secure identity.'

Coping with Wrongs

The family, Christian or otherwise, is not Utopia. Some people have never experienced secure loving family relationships. Others bring to their present family life the hurts and complications from their past experience.

Husbands and wives are not perfect; children are not little angels. Any portrayal of home life that omits wrongdoing is unreal. At one time or another in the average family, there will be: impatience, anger, injustice, laziness, 'little white lies', self-indulgence, self-deception, cunning, bribery—by parents and children alike.

Family life can be hell as well as heaven. But that is not the fault of the structure of the family unit; it is because the unit is made up of people who are fallible. One of the best features of ideal family life is that we, with all our imperfections, may find acceptance and healing within it.

People have to *work* at being a family. Many skills and gifts are needed such as patience, tolerance, the ability to see the other point of view, to know when to compromise, the willingness to forgive. Some learn these gifts and skills as children and adolescents growing up in a family; others have less opportunity to do so, because in their family, problems are more often avoided than solved. If people can only end arguments by slamming the door and storming off to the bedroom or pub, they are practising an avoidance technique in small disputes which, taken to extremes, may one day result in their walking out on their family.

Family life must be looked at honestly. 'Happy families' do not just happen. In a society where many family structures are breaking down, we need to ask, 'Where are people to learn what it takes to create healthy family life?' If it does not happen naturally in a child's own family, then education for family life will have to be provided from outside as a matter of high priority.

'Family life can be hell as well as heaven.'

'People have to work at being a family.'

'… education for family life … a high priority.'

The Summons to Action

This Report is sub-titled 'a crisis of commitment.' There is a human need for love and secure social attachments. That calls for commitment—commitment to those around us, commitment to sharing reliable, unconditional love.

In our society today, there are signs that **many relationships lack commitment**. This lack of commitment is seen in those who:

- live together without the commitment of marriage;
- have a child but don't commit themselves to the other parent;
- marry, but seek release from that commitment in divorce;
- lose contact with their children after divorce.

Children need committed love. It helps build their self esteem, their sense of security, their ability to have faith in someone. It is basic to the future of our society. The changes in our family structures seriously prejudice the chances of our children experiencing that commitment into adulthood. Without it, they have a lesser potential to give committed love themselves.

That crisis of commitment in society calls for commitment from those creating public policy, and also from the Church.

> 'With the steady erosion of relationships in today's world, the church needs urgently to become a visible community, marked by love, God's new society in Christ.'
>
> (Watson)

The Church is called to witness so that people discover the richness of life. The Church is called to explain and to demonstrate the meaning of unconditional love. Many in our society, children and adults, feel pain, because someone close to them has failed to show them committed love. The Church has the potential, in Christ, to be 'channels' of grace, bringing God's love, healing and wholeness.

The law and social provision tend to follow changing social conditions and attitudes. Changes in our family structures are leading to changes in the law. Policy makers still look to the Church for a lead, particularly where family life is concerned. The Church has a responsibility to help raise the consciousness of the nation by taking an active part in public policy debate. The integrity and impact of the Church's response may be the greater if it is possible to combine forces with others who share the Church's concerns.

> 'Policy makers still look to the Church for a lead, particularly where family life is concerned.'

WORKING NOW *for the* FUTURE

7 PUBLIC POLICY

The Board is not alone in suggesting there is a crisis in family matters. Experts in the field draw similar conclusions from the data available. Policy requires more than words; it needs commitment to action within a time scale.

The political parties make statements about children and women, but do not appear to have a coherent family policy. Structuring such a policy is admittedly difficult. There are the personal aspects mentioned on page 6. Any politician will bring to the subject assumptions based on his own family past and present.

There are the complications of co-ordination; family matters cross the divide between various departments and agencies—taxation, education, housing, social work etc—and between private and public law. As a result, bodies charged with considering, say, law reform, may look at issues in isolation, having no remit to consider the tax or social security implications of a proposal.

In formulating policy, as well as tackling weaknesses, it will be important to recognise and play to the strengths of family life, such as the family's role in caring for dependents, young and old, and in asserting the worth of every member.

It will also be important to recognise the variety of families in today's society. Ideally, family policies must be flexible to individual needs and sensitive to different forms of family life. At the same time, the Board emphasises the importance of commending and supporting the Judaeo–Christian ideal of the family—that unit which comprises a mutually committed couple with their children, supported by a wider family.

'Ideally, family policies must be flexible to individual needs and sensitive to different forms of family life.'

Prevention is better (and cheaper) than cure.

We ask public policy makers to tackle four questions:

1 – How should society *support* families, instead of just getting involved as they break down?

There is a need ...to discriminate positively

Marriage and family life need active encouragement and buttressing. This has far-reaching implications for legal, fiscal, economic, educational and welfare policies. Imaginative, family-friendly policies need to be developed.

...to recognise parenting financially

Generally, it has become financially punishing for adults to be part of a family with dependent children. 'The proportion of the gross national product retained by families with dependents is dropping in comparison to those who have no dependents' (Whitfield). It is already accepted by many in Government and elsewhere that in general children fare best in their natural families. If total family breakdown occurs and a child has to be admitted to care, the cost is estimated at some £15,000 per child per year. Yet, since the war, tax benefits for families with dependent children have been eroded and the real value of child benefit has fallen. It now seems that little financial recognition is given to the view that parenting is valuable, productive work.

... to allow for employees' family needs

Employers must achieve greater flexibility in working patterns and employment conditions, for both men and women, not just at the level of paternity and maternity leave but throughout the child-rearing years. The issue of child-care provision needs continuing examination, around such areas as length of time of care per day,

> 'If total family breakdown occurs and a child is admitted to care, the cost is estimated at some £15,000 per child per year.'

> 'Employers must achieve greater flexibility in working patterns and employment conditions ... '

quality of care provided, and continuity of staff providing the care. Scottish local authorities have new responsibilities in these respects as a result of the relevant sections of the Children Act 1989 which came into operation in October 1991. (The rest of this Act applies only to England & Wales.) As Whitfield comments, 'Human resource management must take family dimensions and responsibilities seriously in work scheduling and employee support.'

... to let families choose

Central to issues relating to family matters is the idea of being able to choose how to bring up one's family and not to be forced into, say, poor or inadequate childcare arrangements because of economic necessity. Parents must be given a genuine option for one parent to remain at home to look after the children. Policies and resources need to be directed towards families to offer real choice.

... to support vulnerable families adequately

'Money needs to be targeted to preventative work.'

State and voluntary agencies who have the responsibility for helping troubled families are often severely restricted in funding, particularly with respect to measures aimed at strengthening the family. Often they find themselves reacting to events which have already caused family break-up, rather than giving time and resources to preventative work. Support groups for families and community-run schemes all need funding and can't exist on depleting resources. Money needs to be specifically targeted in these areas.

'Formal education must make a serious attempt to teach about human relationships and the complexities of family life.'

... to educate responsibly

Formal education must make a serious attempt to teach about human relationships and the complexities of family life. Factual education about sex, AIDS *etc* must be linked to such teaching. There must be a concerted attempt to look at responsibilities as well as rights, within marriage, parenthood and family life.

Devising such educational policies is not easy, particularly given adolescent reaction to authority and 'good advice.'

Divorce

2 – How can society balance the need to provide uncomplicated divorce procedures with the need to encourage reconciliation and discourage divorce? The bare statistics indicate the number of couples whose marriages have broken down; they do not reveal the areas of life where the problems arose, or the attempts made to solve them. If divorce became 'easier', then that might demean still further the significance of marriage promises and increase the downward spiral. The divorce process needs a built-in delay, at least for reflection. Many couples might not divorce if counselling were more easily available. It is hard to ensure that that opportunity is given and taken up early enough. It may already be too late when divorce is contemplated. Counselling, which provides the option of improving the couple's relationship, should be available to those 'living together' as well as married.

3 – How can society minimise the ill-effects when a couple do divorce, especially with regard to children? Present divorce procedures encourage each party to consult a separate lawyer so that his/her own 'rights' are best protected. The procedure thereby set in motion is adversarial. Some would argue that this system fuels bitterness, for example in disputes over property and children. In all aspects of divorce, there is a growing need for conciliation, where one 'neutral' person mediates and encourages a couple to reach agreement. Reducing acrimony is important given the indications that children do best if they retain contact with both parents. Funding is needed for conciliation, other services, and research.

> 'Many couples might not divorce if counselling were made more easily available.'

> '... there is a growing need for conciliation ...'

Data

4 – Where is all the data? 'We are going through the fastest change in social relationships in demographic history' (Whitfield).

In compiling this Report, the need for a greater range of statistical and research material has become evident, particularly in relation to the implications of cohabitation. It is important that changes in society are adequately recorded and the data made available. Information from the 1991 census is needed as soon as possible.

Conclusions

The Board urges the creation of policies that commend family life. Already we have discussed the unhappiness and pain that is the result of family break-up. To help families stay together we need to change our thinking on how we structure many of the institutions of our society, so as to protect that which lies at the core of that society, the family. Where a cliff edge is crumbling, the need is not merely for an ambulance at the bottom of the cliff, but for a strong fence at the top.

> 'Where a cliff edge is crumbling, the need is not merely for an ambulance at the bottom of the cliff, but for a strong fence at the top.'

8 The BIBLE—BASIS for a CHRISTIAN RESPONSE

The Bible speaks emphatically on the importance of relationships, commitment and love. As the Panel on Doctrine will be reporting fully on the theology of marriage, the Board gives a simple summary of what the Bible says about God and family life, trying to state principles which Christians would agree as clear Bible teaching.

About God

God is love. In love, God created the world and made humanity, intending people to have a relationship with Himself (1 John 4:7–21). Human beings are more than body and mind; they have a social and a spiritual dimension; they can respond to love and learn to love.

Humanity by disobedience rejected God's love; but God in love did not reject humanity. The intended relationship with God was spoiled, and mere humans could do nothing to restore it (Genesis 3). Even though God was not at fault, He took initiatives to put things right.

In the Old Testament, **God made promises and kept them**, e.g. to Abraham (Genesis 12:1–3). God's certain promise is called a covenant. The prophecy of Hosea shows in graphic form that God keeps loving people even when they reject him. He remains committed. Marriage is a covenant of love; it is a commitment; its promises are meant to be kept.

> 'Marriage is a commitment; its promises are meant to be kept.'

The supreme initiative is revealed in the New Testament: **God went the length of becoming a human being Himself** (John 1:14). In Christ he entered our world of broken relationships, bringing love and healing, sharing with friends their pain in bereavement (John 11:35). Jesus knows how we feel (Hebrews 4:15). As well as being God, Jesus Christ was a fully human being, who shared our sexuality as a male (though there is no indication that he married or expressed his sexuality in intercourse). Jesus was 'despised and rejected,' as predicted in Isaiah 53:3; he deeply understands men and women who have been despised and rejected by others.

God is a reconciling God. Jesus took into himself the consequences of our wrongdoing, to the extent of dying in our place (2 Corinthians 5:21). When we were enemies of God, Christ died for us (Romans 5:6,8,10). The result is that those who accept what he has done can be at peace with God (Romans 5:1). Where there is disagreement in a family, there is a source of reconciliation beyond ourselves—in God and the Gospel.

The God who created can also re-create. Jesus was raised from death to life. His resurrection can give rise to ours (Romans 6:9–11). If anyone is in Christ he is a new creation (2 Corinthians 5:17). There is hope, in marriage as elsewhere. People can change (even the greedy, Luke 19:1–10; and the ruthless, Acts 16:23–34).

'If anyone is in Christ he is a new creation … There is hope, in marriage as elsewhere. People can change …'

In the person of the Holy Spirit, God can live within the believer, giving power beyond one's own (Romans 8:9–14). As a result the believer knows a new level of love, joy, peace, patience and self control (Galatians 5:22).

God is concerned about the way people live. He is just. He is against evil and cruelty. He has a concern for justice, and defends the fatherless and widow, the poor and the immigrant. He is behind laws that protect people from injustice (Romans 13:3,4). He calls on anyone doing wrong to repent, that is, to change (Mark 1:15).

About people

God made humanity male and female (Genesis 1:27). The sexes are different, physically and in other ways, but they are of equal value to God. The differences have to do with reproduction, but also with mutual support. 'It is not good for man to be alone: I will make a helper suitable for him' (Genesis 2:18). Man and woman are interdependent; they are not meant to *compete* with one another, but to *complement* each other.

God's intention for couples is life-long monogamy: one man, married to one woman, until the bond is broken by the death of one or other. Although some men in the Old Testament had multiple partners (e.g. Kings David and Solomon) polygamy is condemned by showing historically its failures, and Deuteronomy 17:17 may be a direct prohibition.

Sexuality is affirmed by God when expressed in marriage. 'A man will leave his father and mother, and be united to his wife, and the two shall become one flesh' (Genesis 2:24). The sexual union is intended to occur after the public events of 'leaving' the dependent state of childhood, and making a commitment to the wife. In the Song of Solomon, the married couple clearly enjoy their intimacy (3:6–5:1). A newly-wed husband was excused army service: 'For one year he is to be free to stay at home and bring happiness to the wife he has married' (Deuteronomy 24:5).

However, some types of sexual behaviour are contrary to the Maker's instructions. God's code of conduct forbids *adultery* (Exodus 20:14), *incest* (Leviticus 18:6–18), *rape and promiscuity*, and clearly expects *virginity until marriage* (Deuteronomy 22). The laws are not merely a matter of morality; deviating from the ideal brings pain; the God of love wishes to spare us that pain. David and Bathsheba's sin of adultery was already unjust, as well as bringing further tragic results including lies and murder (2 Samuel 11). Amnon 'forced' his half sister Tamar (2 Samuel 13); there is revulsion in verses 15,21,22. However, sexual sins could be forgiven, even though the consequences remained (2 Samuel 12:13,14; Psalm 51).

'... deviating from the ideal brings pain; the God of love wishes to spare us that pain.'

Jesus continued the Old Testament emphasis on right conduct in all of life, including sexual matters. He also demonstrated God's forgiveness and compassion. For instance, a woman had been caught in bed with a man not her husband. Some religious people dragged her to Jesus asking his opinion on the appropriate penalty for adultery: 'Moses commanded that such a woman be stoned to death. Now, what do you say?' Jesus by-passed the question, which had no thought for the woman, but was just a trick to see if he would disagree with the Old Testament. It was unjust to demand punishment for the woman but not for the man involved. Jesus challenged their right to apply such a drastic penalty on someone for *this* sin, when they themselves were guilty of *other* sins (cf James 2:10,11). When the accusers, by leaving, had all admitted that they were sinners too, Jesus told the woman, 'Neither do I condemn you,' and added the vital qualification, 'Go, but do not sin again.' Christians aim to pass on that combination of forgiveness and challenge to repentance: to recognise right and wrong, but to do so without repelling the person who, like ourselves, has come short of God's standards in this or any area of life.

Jesus also emphasised the importance of controlling our minds. Not only is the *act* of adultery forbidden; even the *thought* of it is wrong. We ourselves are responsible for banishing any such thought, even if it requires drastic action (Matthew 5:27–30). This passage applies to everyone, whether married or not. In addition to adultery *during* marriage, Jesus condemns the wrong use of sex *prior* to marriage (Mark 7:21–23).

Temptation can be resisted, whether in sexual or other areas of life. Jesus was tempted to misuse his powers, but did not give in (Matthew 4:1–11). Christians can draw on his victory. 'No temptation has seized you except what is common to man. And God is faithful; he will not let you be tempted beyond what you can bear. But when you are tempted, he will also provide a way out so that you can stand up under it (1 Corinthians 10:12).

Jesus shared in the joy of a wedding (John 2) indicating approval for the occasion. A wedding is worth celebrating.

'Temptation can be resisted …
God will not let you be tempted beyond what you can bear.'

The apostle Paul reinforces the Christian ideal of marriage in 1 Corinthians 7. One man marries one woman (verse 2), and they live together in mutual love and support till one of them dies. Sexual relations between them are entirely good and proper, as each recognises the needs of the other (verses 3–5), but the couple must wait till they are married (verse 36), and must abstain completely from intercourse with anyone else (6:18). If a partner dies, the other is free to re-marry—but Christian should marry Christian (verse 39).

Some verses in 1 Corinthians 7 indicate **the option of celibacy**. In Paul's day, Christians expected the Lord to be returning so soon that there was not time for marriage (verse 29). Celibacy is still a valid choice for individuals, but it is not compulsory for anyone (verse 28). The Apostle Peter was married, and Paul claimed the right to be (1 Corinthians 9:5). Candidates for leadership in the Church were to be monogamous (1 Timothy 3:2,12).

'sharing yer piece!— five rolls and two fish'

'Celibacy is still a valid choice for individuals.'

Children matter. Jesus had a special love for children. He experienced childhood himself, including obedience to parents, and he developed mentally, physically, spiritually and socially (Luke 2:40–52). He included children in his healing ministry (Luke 8:40–56; 9:37–43). He delighted in their company (Matthew 19:13), and worked them into his message: 'He ... took a little child and had him stand beside him; then he said to them, "Whoever welcomes this little child in my name welcomes me; and whoever welcomes me welcomes the one who sent me"' (Luke 9:46–48, cf Matthew 18:1–10). He accepted a child's gift of five rolls and two fish and used it to bring blessing to many others (John 6:9). He gave a solemn warning against those who lead children (or new believers) astray

(Mark 9:42). He accepted the praise of children (Matthew 21:15–16). When Jesus was betrayed in the garden, one of his followers was a young man (Mark 14:51).

Relationships in the Christian community were very different from secular society then and now. **Instead of insisting on others giving us 'our rights', Christians were encouraged to fulfil their 'duties.'** The interdependence of husbands and wives is described by different writers in closely similar terms in Ephesians 5:21–33 and 1 Peter 3:1–7. The former sets husbands the incredibly high standard of loving their wives 'as Christ loved the Church.' Paul defines that love by indicating that Christ 'gave his life' for the Church.' When we understand the new relationship with God that emerges by trusting and obeying Jesus as Saviour and Lord, the term translated 'submit', so often misused by men to justify harsh and dictatorial behaviour, takes on a new meaning.

The Christian ideal will not always be easily followed, or commonly accepted in society. 'Brothers, if someone is caught in a sin, you who are spiritual should restore him gently. But watch yourself, or you also may be tempted. Carry each other's burdens, and in this way you will fulfil the law of Christ' (Galatians 6:1,2). 'Do not conform yourselves to the standards of this world, but let God transform you by a complete change of your mind' (Romans 12:2). It will be costly to try to influence others by pointing out that their marriage or family life differs from God's design: when John the Baptist opposed Herod's 'marriage' to Herodias, she had him executed (Mark 6:17–29).

'The Christian ideal will not always be easily followed, or commonly accepted in society.'

9 CHRISTIAN RESPONSES to the CRISIS

Christian Family Lifestyle

Actions speak louder than words. Reports like this achieve little unless the attitudes and actions described can be seen in everyday lives. Christians need to show in their families the 'life in all its fullness' which Jesus came to bring (John 10:10).

Christians have no monopoly on love. Every home displays it in varying degrees; but the Christian home has a standard of love in Jesus, who loved even his enemies. 'Love is patient, love is kind. It does not envy, it does not boast, it is not proud. It is not rude, it is not self-seeking, it is not easily angered, it keeps no record of wrongs. Love does not delight in evil but rejoices with truth. It always protects, always trusts, always hopes, always perseveres' (1 Corinthians 13:4–7). Such a love will show in countless ways.

> 'Christians have no monopoly on love ... but the Christian home has a standard of love in Jesus.'

Children need to grow ... physically

Like every parent, Christians will want to provide for their children's bodily needs: healthy food and drink, warm clothing and shelter, fresh air and exercise, cleanliness, sufficient sleep, preventive and curative medicine. They may limit the size of their family to make sure they can provide for all their children. The work parents do, inside and outside the home, paid and unpaid, is all a sign of love, however much taken for granted.

... intellectually

Christians are just as concerned as other parents for the intellectual development of their children. From earliest attempts at movement and speech, through primary and secondary schooling and possibly tertiary education, parents want each child to go as far as the child is capable. That means parents being involved as far as they are capable, from checking homework to supporting School Boards and giving frequent praise.

... socially

Parents will have time for each other and for their children—or make time. They will do things together, for example eating as a family whenever possible (without distraction from the TV), going out together to visit relations or friends, play sport, attend Church. Such joint activity is the root of social development. We learn to react to others by being with others.

'stretching minds'

Of course, there is always a possibility that two people do not get on. The Christian family should provide the earliest lessons in forgiveness. Pardon is the kind of thing everyone approves of until they themselves are offended. Suddenly they feel, 'But this I can't forgive.' Christians are aware of how many things in their own lives need forgiven by God; they know what it cost Jesus to obtain forgiveness for their sins; and they have his explicit command to forgive as they expect to be forgiven.

... morally

Children need known boundaries. They cannot work out for themselves what is safe, without running the risk of death, from fire, electricity, traffic. Boundaries are also needed in matters of right and wrong. There is a moral dimension to healthy growth. Discipline for crossing the boundaries must always be fair. Penalties must always be appropriate to the understanding of the child, and the extent of conscious disobedience. The New Testament maintains that right discipline is a sign of love, even though human parents can never match the justice of God (Hebrews 12:4–13). Fathers are expressly commanded, 'Do not embitter your children, or they will become discouraged' (Colossians 3:21). This includes knowing when to say no, and when yes to a child's request. It can sometimes be good for children to learn to wait; it prepares them for later life, for example in preventing unnecessary debt, or in keeping sexual intercourse for marriage.

... spiritually

The moral dimension is part of the spiritual. Christians have found a trusting relationship with the God of love. They can't help wanting it for their children. Our loving heavenly Father delights to hear us when we talk to him in prayer, and has lots to say to us in the Bible. There are many books of prayers and Bible excerpts for children of every age. While these are a useful start, we are not limited to printed prayers, but teach conversational prayer by example. To pray aloud with children from infancy (long before they understand the language) allows them to grow up knowing that the God of love is always there, always ready to hear them. Gratitude to God can be expressed with a simple prayer at mealtimes. Christian parents love to gather with God's people in worship on Sundays, taking their children with them. Any inconsistency in attendance at church by one or both parents will be seized upon and copied; merely *sending* children to Sunday School will not last.

> 'Any inconsistency in attendance at church by one or both parents will be seized upon and copied; merely <u>sending</u> children to Sunday School will not last.'

... emotionally

If surrounded by such signs of love, children will grow up in emotional security. Christians are not exempt from suffering. They too face illness, redundancy, unjust treatment and death. Yet the Christian home is meant to be a place of joy and peace. 'My peace I give you ... Do not be afraid' (John 14:27). 'I have told you this so that my joy may be in you and that your joy may be complete' (John 15:11). Such joy is not pious; there should be plenty of exuberant laughter in the Christian life. Home is where tired people relax and unwind. In a truly loving family, there is no need to 'perform' or pretend. We are accepted for what we are, whether we feel up or down.

> 'Christians are not exempt from suffering.'

Family life can be a source of deep, rich emotion, but it can also be place of tyranny and repression, where a parent takes advantage of the children, where a spouse can use sexuality as a bribe or reward for getting their own way. The Christian element may be distorted as parents use an unseen God to threaten children in a terrifying way. A veneer of religious observance or language is no substitute for the gracious service of the God of love.

Husband and wife

Between husband and wife, the commonest expression of love will be in kind deeds and kind words. Their conversation will not stop at passing on news, but will express opinions, and go on to share feelings, confident that they will be heard, taken account of and kept in confidence. A Christian couple will readily discuss decisions to be reached jointly and will not be afraid to disagree. Living together in close proximity, disagreements are inevitable, and can be healthy. The Bible offers a method of resolving differences, big or small. If each partner has found freedom through willing obedience to the Lord Jesus Christ, they can go on to 'be subject to one another out of reverence for Christ' (Ephesians 5:21) (see page 52).

A Christian married couple accept their sexual union as a gift from God. (They do not even consider the possibility of a sexual relationship with anyone else.) Expressing that physical union will be part of a total relationship. There will be many signs of mutual acceptance, care and affection. In tenderly seeking to meet the needs of the other, each partner will find their own fulfilment.

Adults voluntarily choose to place some limits on their own freedom to be themselves so that others can be themselves. Self-sacrifice is a glorious thing when chosen by oneself; it becomes a parody, when others demand it of one. Children can learn it by seeing it in their parents.

The wider circle

People in a Christian home should be interested in the well-being of others. Those who enjoy the blessing of sharing Christian family life must be sensitive to those who do not. By including others, we not only benefit the individual befriended, but also enrich the life of the family itself.

The outward looking attitude will include the couples' parents if still living. The fifth commandment, 'Honour your father and mother ... ' never expires, though there will be different ways of doing so at various stages. The care of elderly people begins with their own children; the attitude we adults show to our parents will affect how our children think of us when we are old. Society's provision for elderly people begins in the family.

'family circle'

The spirit of love will not stop with relations, however. Neighbours come in all shapes and sizes, some living in the same street, others across the world. Our resources are given by the loving God whom we address as 'Our Father'; we cannot forget others who pray to him too. If we have truly learned to share in our family, our giving will show far beyond it. 'We love, because God first loved us' (1 John 4:19).

Young People and Relationships

The Church's responsibility

The Church recognises its particular responsibility towards young people, right from early childhood. That responsibility is perhaps greater than ever, as there is a need to offer young people a perspective on life which will be very different from that offered to them in other quarters. Today's is a materialistic society. Happiness is associated with having. Life gets tough if you cannot have. Happiness is also associated with the instant relationship. Popular literature and the media emphasise romantic and sexual love. They often present the image that it is natural and right for boy and girl to meet, to fall in love and to 'make love.'

If young people are to have an understanding of the complexity and depth of human love and human relationships, then they must grow up learning about it. Specific teaching is called for, but also the 'prayer, precept and example' mentioned at infant baptism. This may not be news, but it is certainly a challenge.

Good books are available (for example *Life in a Sex-mad Society* by Joyce Huggett) and videos (such as *Lessons in Love* by Steve Chalke and Paul Francis—seven talks for the 14–18 age group).

Another way

It is essential to present an alternative to the prevailing social climate, if the devastating effects of active early sexuality and premature sexual relationships are to be avoided. In doing so, the Church must acknowledge that many youngsters will wish to postpone marriage, or 'settling down' with a partner, until their mid-20s when they have completed their studies or experienced life away from home. To many, to wait until then to have a sexual relationship must seem impossibly idealistic. However, we Christians have a responsibility to encourage them to do so.

Going out and 'preaching' to young people is not likely to be a way forward. Before the Church's message will have an impact, individual teenagers will have to see that the Church is interested in them and accepts them for who they are. Personal contacts are essential, whether a young person is already within the Church family or not.

Not alone

Christians do not stand alone. In encouraging Christian teenagers to be 'the lone voice', we must assure them of this. They must know that they belong to a family, the family of God, who will stick with them as they resist the pressures all around to conform. Even more significantly, God, by His Spirit and enabling power, will stand with them and equip them to do His will.

A 17 year old girl wrote to a Christian magazine for help in trying to follow Christian standards. She said she was the only virgin left in her class. She was under pressure from her boyfriend, and the other girls. The editor's answer was a thoughtful one for people in her position, though she might never be able to say it to her friends: 'Any time I want, I can choose to become like you; but you can never choose to go back to being like me.' The difficulty is in speaking to those in her class who have lost their virginity, for whom the advice comes too late. They need to hear about God's forgiveness, but a glib mention of it weakens the support given for those trying hard to maintain Christian standards.

Responses in the Local Church

Raising awareness

An essential part of any response to the crisis is to raise awareness; to help people think about family matters.

It can be difficult to know how to address the issues involved. They may be too personally painful for large group 'instruction', for example from the pulpit. In any group of people there will be some for whom the subject of family life is loaded with pain, past or present.

There is a need for Ministers and congregations to be sensitive to those within or around their congregations. Christ would not have marginalised people because of their family circumstances. In preaching, teaching and sharing together, people's circumstances and needs must be recognised.

Small groups for Bible Study may offer a vehicle for considering the issues. Even there it is not easy for people to talk about their own personal experiences, let alone their inner pain. Everyone

'The issues may be too personally painful for large group "instruction", for example from the pulpit.'

involved may need to be more sensitive to the situation of others, and more honest and vulnerable about themselves. Jesus wants us to know ourselves. In so doing, we may gain a better understanding of the commandment 'Love your neighbour as *yourself.*'

Training

The responsibility for raising awareness about family matters cannot rest only on the laden shoulders of parish ministers. Preaching and teaching in church circles reaches only a small percentage of the population, but if effective could equip church members to contribute sensitively in word and action to many more people around them.

The Church of Scotland already offers commendable training (e.g. through St Ninians, Carberry and St Colms) to help members become more effective in church and community. It is important that courses and materials pay adequate attention to family matters. Christian bookshops carry a range of material under a 'Family Life' heading. Some books focus on particular aspects such husband/wife relationships, bringing up children, life with adolescents, divorce, growing old.

All these tools can help Christians to meet the challenge to teach and live out God's ideal, while showing loving concern for those personally affected by the issues raised.

Acting in response

Christ meets people where they are. So must we as congregations of God's people. We have a responsibility to be alongside the divorcee, the lone parent, the hurt child, demonstrating unconditional love and acceptance, and participating in the practical realities of his or her situation. We are called to love, not to be judgemental. Do we as congregations show the love of Christ? How many congregations know who are lone parents among them or in the parish? Would a divorcee or a single parent be confident enough to disclose that fact or would they fear prejudice? Are we

'We are called to love, not to be judgemental.'

more ready to offer support to a widow than to other lone parents?

Taking action is a responsibility which must be taken up by local congregations and individual members. If someone who trusts us wants to tell us of the experience he or she has been through, or is still living through, and perhaps then to bring it before God, then that is a privilege we share with him or her. Sometimes those most equipped will be members who have had a similar experience themselves, who may have joined together in a self-help group.

'nice to see you, to see you, nice!'

The Board affirms that God's ideal is for all children to live with both their parents throughout their childhood. The Bible commends the importance of nurturing a child. It speaks warmly of relationships of father and child, as well as mother and child. But the Bible is realistic in describing families where these relationships break down. It is important not to marginalise either child or parent in the lone parent situation.

The Board affirms that Christ teaches that marriage is special, that divorce is not the way that He would wish for His people. No-one would wish to 'condemn' someone to stay in a marriage which is beyond redeeming. However, the information presented in this Report demonstrates the implications that the break-up of a family may have for its members and for society at large.

The church has a dual calling—to love and support those for whom the fragmentation of family life is already a reality and to support families and so help prevent this fragmentation. This is a *challenge* to the Church family.

Simple steps—and harder

Simple steps may be greatly helpful. The readiness to be a caring 'neighbour', particularly when families have no relatives nearby. A willingness as individuals or as a congregation to do something practical to ease isolation—for single people, lone parents, new mothers and others—as well as for the elderly and housebound

More demanding may be the need to offer 'unconditional befriending' to someone in difficulties. Some congregations may be able to develop a skilled counselling resource, easing the demands on the already overstretched facilities available elsewhere. Others may encourage members to become trained volunteers with Marriage Guidance, etc. Married couples might be willing to help ministers to provide more comprehensive premarriage courses. Thinking 'family' in congregational life and worship is also important. Church-run 'out of school clubs' may be a real help to families struggling to combine earning with parenthood. Practical help and a listening ear could be offered to individual families going through a stressful period. That could involve going with the person to official appointments; the complexity of the law and the inhibiting nature of official procedures can put many people at a disadvantage.

The Conciliation Service identifies the need for more access centres. These are neutral places where parents can meet or spend time with children who stay with the former partner. Congregations with halls already adapted for a playgroup or creche could offer this facility with minimal upheaval, if they could collect a small rota of responsible adults to staff it. The need is greatest at weekends.

A number of Presbyteries and congregations are already alive to the issues and are offering a response. Some call these 'street level churches' or 'churches with ragged edges', where there is a desire to be closely associated with the needs of the community around.

However, every congregation has great potential to become a resource able to promote the welfare of the families within its parish. Releasing that resource is the *challenge* to prayer and action. The call is to commitment.

In 1981, when the Board last reported to the General Assembly on Family Matters, it endorsed the view that, 'The Christian

'... every congregation has great potential to become a resource able to promote the welfare of the families within its parish.'

community has to become the spear-head of a revolution in comprehending, assisting and safe-guarding all that is best in contemporary marriage' (Dominian). It commented that, 'If the Church is to help people enjoy a deeper experience and understanding of Christian marriage and family life, and produce better models for the world to see of what a joyful and satisfying thing Christian marriage can be, then obviously it must foster the growth of its ministry to couples and families .... In every parish there are couples in need of help and support (now we might say families). This they do not at present always find readily available in the institutional church .... The Church of Scotland has to make up leeway with churches in other parts of the world in its ministry to married couples and the family.'

Ten years on, the Board repeats that statement. Another ten years on, will another 'rallying call' have to be made? By then, the fragmentation of our family structures will be even more evident.

Ministers and Marriage

Communication

Sunday school teachers have long been aware that they cannot merely refer to God as 'Father'; they first need to tell a story describing a happy and secure family with a loving father. In much the same way, ministers interviewing couples who come to ask for a church wedding need to take part in a discussion of what a good relationship is. We can no longer assume that they share Christian goals, standards or language.

Remarriage of divorcees

With the increase in the number of couples seeking weddings where one or other has previously been divorced, there is a growing pressure on ministers to officiate as a matter of course. It is necessary to reaffirm the position of the Church of Scotland expressed in Act 26, 1959: 'A minister shall not accede as a matter of routine.'

> 'If the Church is to help people enjoy a deeper experience and understanding of Christian marriage and family life ... then obviously it must foster the growth of its ministry to couples and families.'

> 'We can no longer assume that couples share Christian goals, standards or language.'

Christians agree that Jesus regretted divorce, seeing it as a concession which fell short of the ideal given by God at creation. However, some think he did allow it, and remarriage thereafter; others think that if he accepted divorce, he did not allow remarriage. In 1 Corinthians 7, Paul allowed for the possibility of divorce in certain circumstances. Some think he thereby allowed remarriage, while others think he explicitly excluded it. Proponents of both views are aware that God's forgiveness must also be taken into account.

Given this breadth of honestly and deeply held opinion, the General Assembly included clause 6: 'A minister shall not be required to solemnise a re-marriage against his conscience.' The Board believes it is important to retain this clause.

In addition to matters of conscience, some ministers feel that every time they ask a divorcee to re-take vows meant to last 'till God shall separate us by death', they devalue the meaning of the words for first-timers.

Ministers need a simple message for divorcees. The Act requires the minister to ascertain that there has been 'sincere repentance where guilt has existed in the past on the part of any divorced person seeking re-marriage.' However, when a couple appear out of the blue, it is almost impossible for the minister to discover this within the timescale demanded by them: they usually want a quick answer on the wedding *date* to let them book the reception.

Even where a minister does not in general object to remarrying a person after a first divorce, there is need for fresh guidance for when a person has been married more than once before, and for situations where previous relationships involved no weddings, but only cohabitation(s).

Intercourse before marriage

Ministers also need to take note of the very high level of pre-marital intercourse. In the 1979 *Book of Common Order*, the wedding service omitted a phrase previously used: 'Let us invoke the blessing of God on the union now to be formed', and inserted: 'Let us ask God's blessing on this union.' It may be more honest to provide a church service which asks a blessing on the existing union now being acknowledged.

Ministers want to offer pre-marriage counselling. Some do not raise the issue of sex before marriage, or do so only in a general way, and take no action if a couple admit to it. Others feel obliged to go much further. Seeing all intercourse outside of marriage as sinful, they may ask the couple if they are observing Christian standards in their relationships, and if not, to repent, that is, to refrain from intercourse till the wedding. Or they may agree to conduct a ceremony, but at a much closer date than the twelve months notice commonly dictated by hotel bookings. Their intention is to regularise and acknowledge the relationship already begun. They believe there can be no sense of forgiveness till there is admission of a need for it.

> 'Ministers need to take note of the very high level of premarital intercourse ... the issues are not easy.'

These issues are not easy. Two case studies may show some of the complexity:

Example A

A couple get married in church. Neither is in consistent paid work; they live in poverty. The wife experiences violence from the husband and leaves; he resists divorce. Before the five years are up, she enters a new relationship, and two children arrive. She and her new partner attend church.

Throughout that time the church continues to be alongside them, demonstrating unconditional love, participating in the horror and terror of the situation. The central strategy has been to affirm their worth in the eyes of God, accepting them where they are, rather than where we would like to see them, a determination to bring down barriers. The past six years have been about grappling with where their situation is, encouraging them towards the rites of marriage based on a celebration of their current commitment.

Example B

At the second meeting of a communicants' class (topic: sin and God's forgiveness) someone asks why Jesus in Mark 7:14–23 lists both adultery and sexual immorality. The minister explains: 'Adultery' means sex by a married person with someone not their spouse: 'sexual immorality' is wider, covering all wrong use of sex, including sex before marriage.

After the class has left, a woman speaks to him in tears. Her parents are both dead. Her boyfriend has moved in with her. They want to marry with God's blessing but can't afford an early wedding. The minister finds it difficult to suggest separating till the wedding, as that would make the boyfriend homeless. Before the next interview, the minister lends a book commending chastity before marriage and ways of achieving it. The woman opts to refrain from sexual intercourse and to sleep in separate rooms till the wedding. The man agrees to try. The minister agrees to marry them, and prays with them for God's forgiveness and help. Months later he conducts a happy, honest ceremony. The wife still attends church.

The Board does not doubt the loving motives of the ministers in these cases, but has no evidence about the long term effects of differing policies. Do ministers in category A give the impression that there is nothing wrong with sex before marriage? Do couples with a minister in category B get the intended message about the seriousness of disobeying God and the joy of forgiveness and new life, or do most just reject minister, Church and God for ever? Research within the Church is needed.

A Response from the Central Church

The subject matter of this Report is basic to the future of our society. Family issues link to almost all the other major issues of the day:

- child abuse and protection;
- homelessness;
- care of elderly people;
- male and female roles;
- changing employment patterns;
- poverty.

There is an urgent need to recognise the trends; to challenge people with the evidence and to stimulate action to uphold what is vital and good about family relationships. That action is needed quickly if it is to build up momentum in time to halt and turn the tide. It must not be restricted to support after a relationship is broken; it must also be preventive.

'Urgent action is needed to uphold what is vital and good about family relationships.'

Key

The Church has a key role to play. Here's why:

- Debate and action on the family have a spiritual dimension;
- The Church of Scotland, with its parish network, has the potential for 'grass roots' involvement throughout Scotland, tailored to suit the needs of a community, individual congregations and families;
- The Church has two priceless resources—people and prayer. Prayerful, loving people with commitment and understanding can be given appropriate training. We cannot leave things to the State or Social Work Departments, already struggling to make the most effective use of their limited resources;
- The Church has the benefit of the Holy Spirit to enable and empower its work and the individual members involved. The

'The Church has two priceless resources— people and prayer.'

page 67

Church is challenged to show the concern and the active, committed love that Jesus Himself demonstrated.

'You are my family'

Much valuable work is already being done at Parish level, quietly, unheralded. Clearly, more is needed. The Board's staff are looking to see if there are ways of supporting local initiatives in this area, conscious of the overlap with other Boards of the Church.

This Report suggests that there is great potential for local congregations to become involved not only in accepting, loving and helping families with specific difficulties, but also in expressing love, support and a sense of belonging to the 'ordinary' family—to be living, caring Christian families within the larger Church family. That call extends too to the person 'without' a family of their own, for whom there may become a real sense that 'you, the people of the Church, are my family now.'

> 'Family life is the best if imperfect vehicle we have for developing personal security, educational support, individual responsibility and social harmony. If we do nothing coherent to buttress family life, then still further increases in domestic turmoil, child insecurity and social disorder are inevitable; and the process will be cumulative.'
>
> (Whitfield)

Appendix

Acknowledgements

The Board thanks the following guests who addressed the Study Group:
- Dr Eric Clive, Scottish Law Commission
- Right Rev. Mario Conti, Roman Catholic Bishop of Aberdeen
- Dr Bob Holman, FARE project, Easterhouse, Glasgow, former Professor of Social Work, Bath
- Ms Susan Matheson, Scottish Association of Family Conciliation Services
- Rev. James Philip, Holyrood Abbey Church of Scotland, Edinburgh
- Dr Gordon Wenham, College of St Mary & St Paul, Cheltenham
- Professor Richard Whitfield, Chairman, National Family Trust, former Dean of Social Sciences and Humanities, University of Aston, and Emeritus Professor of Education
- Very Rev. James Whyte, Emeritus Professor, St Andrews

Sources quoted

- *General Household Survey* 1988 and 1989 (HMSO)
- Registrar General Scotland *Annual Report* 1990
- Argyle, M. and M. Henderson: *The Anatomy of Relationships* (Penguin: 1985)
- Holloway, Richard: *Paradoxes of Christian Faith and Life*
- Kruck, Edward: *The Impact of Divorce on Non-custodial fathers*, quoted by Anne H. Dick, Chairman of the Family Law Association in *Journal of the Law Society of Scotland* April 1991
- Mitchell, Ann: *Children in the Middle. Living through Divorce* (Tavistock: 1985)
- Schaffer, H Rudolf: *Making decisions about Children; Psychological Questions and Answers* (Basil Blackwell: 1990)
- Watson, David: *I believe in the Church* (Hodder and Stoughton: 1978)
- Whitfield, Richard: *Family Policies or social collapse* (Crossbow: Summer 1989)
- Whitfield, Richard (ed): *Families Matter—Towards a programme of action* (Marshall Pickering: 1987)

Other selected bibliography

- Scottish Law Commission: *The effects of cohabitation in private law*
- Scottish Law Commission: *Parental responsibilities and rights, guardianship and the administration of children's property*

- National Family Trust: *Learning to love; Facing up to family income* (101 Queen Victoria Street, London EC4P 4EP)
- Reports to the General Assembly on related topics:
    Board of Social Responsibility
        Abortion (e.g. 1985; 1986; 1987; 1988)
        AIDS (1987 pages 320–327; 1988; 1989; 1991)
        Childlessness (1980–82; 1985)
        Child Abuse 1990
        Divorce (1967–82)
        Ritual Abuse 1991
        Sexuality 1983
    Church and Nation Committee
        Poverty (1982; 1983; 1987; 1989–91)
        Committee on *Women and Men in Society* (1978–80)
- *Keeping Body and Soul Together*, Report to the Presbyterian Church (USA) 1991.

Material for young people

- Huggett, Joyce: Life in a Sex-Mad Society (IVP: 1988)
- Chalke, S and P Francis: Lessons in Love, video for 14-18 years (CARE for the Family, 53 Romney Street, London SW1P 3RF)

Composition of Study Group

The study group began with five women and four men. There was a slight change in personnel after the first year, which necessitated a change of Convener. Skills represented for one or both years included: a theologian, two Parish ministers, a community minister, an Emeritus Professor of Medicine, a solicitor and four social workers. One of the social workers is the Principal Child Care Officer for a Scottish Region, another worked with the Scottish Council for Single Parents. Two of the women are single; the other three, and all of the men, are married.